WAYS TO GET
SPEAKING
ENGAGEMENTS

7

WAYS TO GET

SPEAKING ENGAGEMENTS

7 Ways to Get Speaking Engagements

Ordering Information:
Special discounts are available on quantity purchases by corporations, associations, and others. For ordering details, contact the publisher at the website or email address listed.

Website: **SuccessSpeaksGlobal.com**

Email: info@SuccessSpeaksGlobal.com

Success Speaks Global
2770 Main Street – Suite 147
Frisco, TX 75033

Printed in the United States of America.

TABLE OF CONTENTS

LET ME
COUNT THE WAYS

I am a microphone magnet. I love it. It seems that every room I go into, eventually a microphone gets passed to me. It's not because I'm eager. It is not because I'm desperate. Utilizing these seven ways, I'm going to show you how a microphone gravitates to me.

I am encouraging you to be authentic. I don't try to be anybody else. I use my personality and my sense of humor. I have a theater history, so that's why I'm expressive. People often say that my face tells it all. Sometimes, I talk with my hands. I tried to change it, but now I have grown to accept it. My audience loves it and so do I!

Even though we can be trained on stage decorum and the technical parts of speaking, I encourage you to be your true self; a person of authenticity. There are people out there who do not fit the status quo of traditional speakers. Guess what? Not only do they have amazing careers, they are turning down offers because they are in such high demand.

That's what people are looking for now—authenticity. So, fluff be gone! Let's uncover seven ways to get speaking engagements.

Rekesha Pittman

Success Speaks Global

HOST EVENTS

This works for me time and time again. Don't ask anyone else to book you to speak if you won't book yourself! Host events. These include workshops, seminars and conferences. I have done them all.

WORKSHOPS

If you are emerging as a new speaker, host a workshop in a professional setting. Workshops can be anywhere from 1-2 hours, or 4 hours if you want to do half a day. Focus on your field of expertise and where you are respected and have a lot of information. There are lots of coworking spaces available that you can rent without having to risk a whole lot of money going into a hotel scenario, which can get costly. You can rent hotel space if you'd like, but since small business and startups are currently celebrated, I would look into securing meeting space in one of those facilities.

I am in one now. My monthly membership includes a certain number of hours that I can utilize to host events at no additional charge. If you are not a member of one, there are membership levels you can get with or without an office or you may be able to request non-member rental rates for relatively low-cost event space. You may select a meeting room or a boardroom. Say, "I have 20 tickets available," and sell it out.

Plan a workshop featuring yourself. You can also solicit testimonials from people who attend. Gather both video and written testimonials from attendees, if possible. This allows you to test your content so that when you get to a larger, broader audience, you are more confident.

Bring an assistant or a friend along to take pictures and record video of you in action. The reason I suggest this is because you can have someone take pictures while you are speaking. These images can be used to promote upcoming appearances or for branding purposes. Be strategic about your look. Use photos from the event as social proof that you're hosting events, seminars, panels, or networking gatherings. You can have materials to distribute along with your contact information.

CONFERENCES

Hosting a conference can get expensive depending on what type of program you're planning. Some events will require a larger financial investment. This is exactly how I became a professional speaker—I sponsored the events myself. I was still working full-time in Corporate America when I started.

My first events were dance conferences. I spent from about $2,000 to $4,000 per year to host a "free" conference. It was free for *them*, but not for me. Registration included a free lunch. People often say, "There's no such thing as a free lunch." That's because someone else was paying for it! I provided lunch and also had a concert at the end for guests to participate.

If you have a way for people to interact, it may be of more value to them for the time spent. You offer registrants some type of incentive for attendance—prize drawings, bonuses, giveaways—something that you can use to encourage them to actually show up. Sometimes events that are complimentary result in a larger percentage of no-shows because they do not feel obligated to attend. Absolutely offer them something to follow through. This is a great way to build your marketing list for the future.

Consider any self-sponsored events a marketing investment for your speaking career. You're building an army of loyal followers so that you can gain other sponsors and supporters who would like to partner with you based on the number of people who attend your events.

The first event I hosted was standing room only and the word quickly spread around town. Since I was a featured speaker, I landed additional opportunities and invitations to present—almost too many!

The following year, the house was packed again. My reputation as a speaker and event host was established and official. Some might not agree with this method, but I'm telling you what has worked for me. I was able to break into the speaking arena and become very confident in front of large crowds of people.

Maybe you feel like an introvert. I would advise you against placing these labels on yourself, okay? After all, speaking, is about **reach**. There are people who specifically need to hear from you. If you start to stick all of these limiting labels on yourself, it hinders you. Don't.

I have said this before, and I will say it again: when I enter a room, I had to stop thinking about how people make me feel. Instead, I started thinking about how I make other people feel when I enter a room. Do I make it more valuable or am I a liability to that room? I will work the heck out of a room.

When you go into a room, what do you bring? Do you bring a smile? Do you bring a greeting? Add value to the room and watch yourself bloom.

BUILD AN ONLINE PRESENCE

I know some of us do not have a ton of time to engage in social media. But I will tell you this, if you make it a part of your plan, it will work. Social media is a part of your speaking package.

I have landed multiple speaking engagements because of my famous (or infamous depending on what you think) live videos. As a result of these videos, several event hosts reached out to me via inbox or email to book me to speak. I received an offer to write for a newspaper because of my Facebook Lives and written posts. I had my own column for two years in that publication.

If you are a speaker who wants to be paid to speak, how you present yourself online matters. You may not want to accept this, but Mark Zuckerberg does not look at Facebook like "It's just my personal page." Get rid of that way of thinking and allow it to work to your advantage. Build an online presence.

If I am being pitched a potential speaker by my team or partners, you best believe that I went to look at their social media profile immediately. Either I chuckled or I was impressed. Okay, so bill, I know you laugh.

Really think about your social media. Consider the images that you use. Are they out of date or unprofessional? Think about the content that you put out there... is it relevant to your speaking career?

Put a strategy in place for your social media, even if you just take four hours per month and hammer out a bunch of different photos and posts that will garner respect for what you do and attract the right audience.

If you want to schedule your posts, that's okay. But don't be missing in action. Don't be a ghost. Don't disappear and then wonder why nobody's calling you to speak. Well, nobody knew you were home!

Build a presence via social media whether it's Facebook, Twitter, Instagram, Snapchat, or other emerging platforms. Facebook works wonders for me. On Instagram, people DM me and they do want to connect. I have gotten speaking engagements based off of my Instagram profile alone. I am definitely thinking about the pictures that I post, my video quality and the kinds of content that I put out there. I encourage you to be strategic also.

Do you have a website? Do you? Do you own the "virtual real estate" address that is connected to your name? If you have a more common name, try to be creative or add a word in the front or the back to make it yours. I know my name is a little more unique, but I own my name in multiple formats: RekeshaPittman.com, Rekesha.com and BooksByRekesha.com

Make sure that you have some type of online presence in addition to your social media pages. If you have been sitting on a parked domain, built it up. Even if it's a one pager, build it. Create something nice. Do not feel like you need to have 10 pages of content.

At least have an amazing professional photo. Where are your branded, casual, and unfiltered photos? You need all of them.

Do you look like a good investment? Do you look like a **vault**? Do you look like a place where people feel safe not only to place their money with you, but lend you their trust? Sometimes impressions go beyond money. Make yours count in your favor.

Have a great bio ready to go at all times. Please know this: some people put too much information in their bios. We don't need your whole entire résumé, but we need what's relevant. Include what validates you, certifies you, affirms you, compliments you.

Throw away that same old boring bio that you've been using far too long. Maybe you need to engage the services of a copywriter or someone who knows how to market and craft a compelling bio. Your accomplishments and impact should shine.

Start somewhere, but upgrade as you go. I have invested in a webcam and a ring light. I purchased a Bluetooth microphone for my computer so that the quality of what I record is better than what my standard computer can offer. Think about those things. I have tripods and I make sure that I have a good phone that I can use when I'm on the road or I am on the go. When I go live, I have a purpose. I want to be confident that when I put something out there it is worth watching.

No shade to any other types of phone users, but if you're going to go walk and talk, can you not pixelate and can you not be all fuzzy? That's all I'm saying. Make sure that your videos are good, whether they are live videos or pre-recorded footage.

You can do live videos and place them on social media, video hosting services and your own website. If your technology skills are up to the challenge, you can edit snippets of videos and create several separate posts from the same footage. The algorithm favors live videos with interaction. If you're going to tackle video (and you should), do it consistently and do it well.

You cannot be "virtually homeless," if you are serious about building an online presence. When you use it right, you can land speaking engagements

NETWORK

This is another thing that I think people miss out on. Attend events! Go out. Dress up. Speak and smile. Rinse and repeat.

Be prepared to exchange information. I carry physical business cards (they still work in many cases) and I also send digital business cards via a free app on my phone. The good thing about using my digital card is that I can generate different versions and send the most relevant one. The digital card app allows me to include my picture, phone number, email address, website, and a physical business location. You can include as much or as little information as you'd like for each organization and text it to anyone.

Using a digital card has enhanced my networking efforts, even in informal situations. I was standing in line at the airport on my way to New Jersey. I made some small talk with someone who asked what I did for a living. He asked me if I had a card so that he could refer clients to me. I asked him for his number and sent the information instantly.

I understand that networking opportunities are everywhere, so I always try my best to look professional, especially when I travel. Your next business partner might be waiting in an airplane seat near you!

Attend events with a strategy in mind. Don't be the type of person who goes to events and pushes hard to sell something or tries to land a speaking opportunity immediately. Make an effort to get to know people and find out what they may need.

Who is your ideal crowd? Those are the people you should connect to and spend the most time with. My ideal contacts are entrepreneurs, professionals and motivated go-getters. Creatives are also good to know. So, I have to go to events—whether they are free networking events or paid—to meet people.

Another way that I network is through event registration. I usually bypass general registration and select VIP or tickets with extra perks. It may cost a little extra, but I have found that I am usually sitting next to decision-makers and other people who don't mind spending a little money to get into the right rooms. I have landed several speaking engagements meeting people this way. It's not the money, but the mindset that I aim for. I don't necessarily try to impress or meet a speaker on the platform, especially if it's a celebrity event. If you like to take photos, with influencers, great! There is always someone ready to ask celebrities for favors. I choose to find the hidden gems.

The people sitting next to me have made an investment in themselves. Many of them also host events and understand the power of networking. Many events that offer VIP registration have a special networking party, VIP room, or exclusive sessions for connection purposes.

Every single year, I attend at least one major event that requires some level of investment in order to network with high-level performers. That is a price that I am willing to pay.

Virtual networking has also worked wonders for me! I utilize apps and websites like Shapr, Alignable and MeetUp to connect with others remotely. I like to video chat first before I agree to meet anyone face-to-face.

I use Shapr on a daily basis. It is like "business dating" without the romance. It matches you to people in your local area and abroad with similar business interests. When I travel, the list of potential connections changes to the location I am in! Don't be scared. It does not give strangers your address. This can help you connect with people while you are in the area, especially if you are staying there for a few days. You can only communicate when both parties indicate a mutual interest in meeting. There is a limit to how many people you can potentially connect on Shapr with each day and the batch refreshes every 24 hours.

I was hosting an Author Expo and used Shapr while on the road. Someone I matched with had a friend who wanted to publish a book. I was able to give him information about the expo location. Guess what? He came and brought a friend along! A valuable connection was made. This would not have happened had I not been networking daily.

Yes, I have received speaking engagements as a result of using Shapr.

Even if you don't like to take chances with random networking events, embrace the value of networking in various ways. You don't have to creep in people's inboxes on social media. There are people waiting for you to add as much value as you seek who are waiting to hear you speak.

Way 4

VOLUNTEER

This is a **BIG** winner for me. In case you did not know, this is this is one of my success secrets. I don't tell everybody about this strategy, but this works if you want to land speaking engagements: Volunteer!

Let me tell you how to land a speaking engagement by volunteering. I volunteer for high-profile events for several reasons. Since I am conscious about how I present myself, I never fail to get the attention of whomever is in charge. This person can be the visionary of the event or the leader in charge of the volunteers. All I know is, I'm going to go in there and shine!

I volunteer and also pay for registration. I am not there to attend for free. I am there to position myself. Once, I volunteered to serve at a major Hollywood event in Los Angeles where super-duper mega celebrities were scheduled to attend. As my microphone magnetism would have it, I ended up moderating a leaders-only panel at the same event where very famous people were hosting panels. I am not saying that volunteerism will guarantee a speaking spot, but I would not have had the microphone if I had not.

Since I also host events, I volunteer at successful gatherings to see how they organize their backstage work, conduct meetings, and handle special guests. I apply what I learn to rave reviews.

If you can, find a high-profile event to volunteer for but don't go in there acting like a fan. This may require some travel if these events are scarce in your location. Consider it research for your speaking career. Become a good student.

I signed up to help at a major event held in an arena featuring a very well-known speaker. They assigned me to the bookstore. I learned techniques about organizing, sales strategies, and how to set up my own speaker booth by observation.

Beyond events and conventions, I volunteer with membership organizations. Even if I have to pay to participate, I always find out how I can help. Do you realize how many speaking invitations I received as a result?

Lots! I am the one who asks the leader, "Is there anything I can help you with?" I roll up my sleeves and get to work. The next thing I know, I am being asked to introduce someone or make an announcement over the microphone. Next, my face ends up on a flyer. Get it?

This may work if you know you have a spirit of excellence. When I show up, I look polished. It's not always about wearing professional attire, because it depends on where you're going, but I stay ready. I smile and making people feel comfortable.

As a volunteer, you won't get a whole lot of talking or pushback from me. I am there to absorb and prepare myself for any opportunity that is meant for me. I'm gonna share something with you right now, if you volunteer with me on a regular basis, I will probably give you a speaking engagement. Many others operate the same way. Be help to get help.

EMCEE OR MODERATE

Emcee or moderate, even if you are not a main speaker. Serving as an emcee or panel moderation is a great introduction to speaking. I've read speaker bios, hosted panels, and facilitated roundtable discussions.

If you can move a program along and know how to move the crowd, you can use this to your advantage. Having a sense of humor helps. Make sure that people can feel your positive energy throughout the room. **Energy** a word that people use to describe what they experience in my presence. You need energy. So, turn it on—even if you're not feeling your best. Give the room more than you need from it.

Develop the skills to keep a panel moving even if you received the questions in advance. If the schedule permits, give people time to ask questions. Acknowledge and thank any panelists by name afterwards (and be sure to pronounce them right!).

Spectators may approach you to talk. Thank each and every individual and shake their hands if you can. People do remember how you make them feel.

I moderated an event recently. During the break, I walked around to individual tables and thanked people for showing up. You know what that did? It helped me to establish a rapport with them. So, who are they going to think about when they host a similar event? Me!

I admit that interacting did not come naturally for me and I don't always want to be around a bunch of people. Being a loner did not work to my advantage.

We often label ourselves with titles like introvert, extrovert, etc. If you call yourself an introvert, peel off that label and throw it away! What I am encouraging you to do is go in there and make it your job to make the room feel better.

If you are holding a microphone in your hand or if you are standing at the podium, people will assume that you are in some type of leadership role. So, go ahead, smooth out any feathers in advance. Genuinely connect with people and some may tell you how they really feel. You can carry that feedback forward or tuck it down on the inside so that when you are hosting your own events, the experience will work in your favor. Accept these types of opportunities and watch yourself move up the speaking ladder.

CREATE PARTNERSHIPS

Partnerships work if your audience alone is not large enough to fill a room. For the type of engagements that you desire, try to partner up with another speaker (or group of presenters) and bring those audiences together.

TOURS

If you want to form speaker partnerships, you can take several different approaches. You can organize regional tours. Let's say that you and a couple of your friends all live on the East Coast, you can do a smaller three-city tour. It may not be the same weekend or month, but you can schedule dates in the summer and speak in each or your local areas. You can select a particular subject and promote the tour. You can each get a chance to speak and triple up on your marketing efforts.

If one person in a city has a following and the other speakers in the group are new to that area, it helps everyone build a larger following. This increases the number of speaking engagements for that year and lends credibility to each of you as professional speakers.

If you see me in Atlanta, New Jersey, New York, Texas, California, Louisiana and so on and so forth, then that shows that I'm in-demand. I would create advertisements for each stop and promote them on social media and via my subscriber lists.

SEMINARS AND WORKSHOPS

Co-hosting seminars and/or workshops via partnerships also works. If there is someone in your area who may want to speak on a panel, conduct a workshop, or present a seminar, you may agree to do it one time only to see if you are a good fit for the future.

I hosted an entrepreneurial mastermind with a partner. I utilized my skill set, she brought her abilities to the table, and we put them together. We traveled to Maui, Hawaii for an amazing event and formed some great relationships. It would not have worked if it was just me. It would not have worked if she had done it alone, but because we both have strengths that work well together, we were able to host a successful event. Her skills are great and my skills are great, yet they're different. Together, we're pulling in an audience.

All partnerships are not created equal. Seek capable co-hosts but make sure that you both are doing the work. Carrying dead weight in marketing and promotions can make you want to cancel the date!

SPONSORSHIPS

I know that you want to get paid to speak—we all do—but sometimes you can sponsor in order to speak. If you pay a designated amount of money to sponsor an event, some event organizers will offer you a workshop, special presentation, or a featured speaking engagement. You may also get a booth and an opportunity to meet and collect information from attendees. Some businesses do this often.

If you are trying to build a speaking platform, or if you're trying to get in front of prominent people, you need to show up and you need to get a microphone in your hand. You may have to invest in your own exposure. Don't feel any kind of guilt about it, and when you do, come with your A-game! Make sure that your collateral and pictures are amazing. Have a professional display that includes retractable banners, pop-up banners—whatever you prefer.

I will add light and all kinds of visually appealing décor to get people to come to my speaker table. Excellence attracts. When I have a booth and I know that it's a major event with anywhere from 500 people to 1000 plus, I will turn that booth out. I plan my booth for at least six months in advance to gather the materials I need. The goal is not to be competitive, but to position myself for greater opportunities.

Don't think that you have to do it all at once. Plan for it. When you show up, show all the way out!

PUBLISH A BOOK

Speakers need books. Do you really need to be convinced of this? Publishing opens up speaking doors because people want to hear the author. They want to meet the author and they want signed copies of the book.

Very early in my author career, I did a book signing at a local library. Patrons wanted to meet me simply because I published a book. The library promoted it to their database and I invited my supporters. I was able to bring snacks and read excerpts from my book and sell it.

Books also open up media opportunities. I've had TV appearances in talk show format and multiple news appearances. I go on radio frequently. When I'm at the radio station, I stream the video live to my social media platforms. I carry a little tripod or something to set my phone on to keep my hands free. When people see me on TV or hear me on the radio, it validates my expertise. I have also been featured in newspapers, magazines, and online media outlets.

What will people say when they see me in the media? "Oh, she's on the news." "She's on the radio." "She's a professional." "Book her to speak."

Social media can be a powerful tool for authors who speak. You can read excerpts of your book on social media and discuss topics with your viewers. You can also schedule video interviews or be interviewed by other people on social media, and talk about your book.

When people hear you, it is different than reading about you. It is different than seeing a picture of you; they get to connect *with* you. Don't run from social media. Use it to speak to eager listeners.

There are people who have not met me in person but they follow me on social media. As soon as they meet me, they say that they feel like they already know me because they've heard me speak before. Since I've already established a real connection with them, who are they going to think about when they're hosting an event?

Publish a book that will solidify you as an expert. I host several author expos each year. Because people published books, they were able to get on the platform with me and speak to the audience. I was able to ask them questions. When they held the microphone and spoke about their material, there were other people in the audience watching who were compelled to buy their books. This type of exposure can open additional doors for authors to speak.

Book signings can be very effective for speakers. You can host your own book signing, and plan a speaking tour for yourself. It may take work to market it, but capturing video and photos of people with your book in their hands is valuable social proof.

I release at least one new book every single year. This keeps my subject matter fresh. Since I visit certain markets each year, it also gives me something new to discuss with the media.

I started out speaking and publishing books in the arts arena. I am no longer as prominent in that area, but because of my extensive collection of books on the subject, I am still in demand in that community.

Even though I'm not primarily engaged in the arts, because of my years of publishing and speaking history, I am still viewed as an expert and people still bring me out to speak.

I released several books about publishing and spoke all over the world about it. In 2018, I released a book on business. Why? People in business were inviting me to speak in business arenas, but not about publishing. They wanted to hear about my journey as an entrepreneur. So, being the smart business-woman that I am, I said, "Let me write a book for this arena so that when I go to speak at business conferences, I'm not pigeonholed as a publisher." It worked.

Release a relevant book. It is a valuable marketing tool. It is a résumé of your exper-tise. Authorship is absolutely wonderful for your legacy.

Produce new material often. Don't be stuck with a book that you released five years ago. Write a new one, especially if you want to speak. Either write a book for an arena that is calling for you or develop a book for an arena that you want to get into. Even if no one is asking yet, if you want to get into a new sector, write a book about it and watch doors open

You can also align yourself with causes through your book. I have authors who write books about domestic violence and speak for organizations that are advocates for women's rights and anti-domestic abuse.

If you're going to write a book, try to see which organizations can endorse your subject matter. Reach out to them, but don't promote your book and speaker booking information immediately. Connect with key organizational advocates and leaders where possible. Ask if there is anything you can do to support the cause. If the conversation so happens to go the book route, that is fine. You can then transition into an opportunity.

There are certain months throughout the year designated for awareness. Look at a calendar to research what is going on each month and strategically plan your book promotions so that you can be considered as an event speaker. Titans in business publish often. You should too.

STEP UP TO THE MIC

All of these strategies are useless without a relevant message. Becoming a speaker is not about fame, celebrity, or money, but about making an impact. I always say, "My outcome justifies my income." No one wants to be bored when hearing someone speak. Use your platform to make a difference.

Know what is happening in the world around you. Learn about different cultures and emerging issues. You don't have to be in politics to understand that words can be polarizing. If you want to be controversial, do it, but understand what you are doing and your endgame.

Get rid of your insecurities (that voice in your head is not always right), and be confident that there are people in this world whose ears are calibrated to your unique voice. If there are successful speakers without limbs who travel all over the world, why can't you? Our limitations are only what we allow them to be.

Maintain your creative edge. Improve your presentations. Don't just throw a slide show together and hope for the best. Invest in your toolkit as a speaker and watch the crowd clamor for more.

Being popular does not justify rude behavior. Try to be as gracious as you can. People may get emotional in response to something you say. Allow them to have a moment. Everyone will not agree with you. You may be misunderstood and misquoted from time to time. Relax. It comes with the territory.

If you desire bigger opportunities as a speaker, practice. Study psychology. Read sales books. Develop products and services. Build a thriving community that embraces your philosophies. Remain open and teachable.

I have included several resources on the next few pages that I believe will be useful for you. As your speaking opportunities increase, feel free to reach out to me with the good news!

SPEAKER RESOURCES

SUCCESS SPEAKS GLOBAL

Success Speaks Global is not just another speaker association. SSG is a community of active and growing speakers across the globe who are interested in securing valuable speaking opportunities, creating multiple revenue streams, and expanding their reach across worldwide. This is achieved through online support, strategic resources, regional meetings, and an annual speaking competition. Members receive benefits including:

- **Accelerated Training** (Media, Technique, Marketing, Online Resources)
- **Access to Exclusive Speaking Opportunities**

- **Eligibility for Annual Success Speaks Competition** (Cash and Prizes Awarded)
- **Featured Speaker Eligibility** (SSG Online Magazine)
- **Complimentary eBooks**
- **Mastermind Opportunities**
- **Reserved Members-Only Seating at Events**
- **Exclusive Registration Discounts and Early Access**
- **Exclusive Member Swag**

Membership Levels:

Emerging – Essential – Expert – Executive

Profit-sharing opportunities available!

SuccessSpeaksGlobal.com

SUCCESS SPEAKS
E.A.S.T.

SUCCESS SPEAKS E.A.S.T

Go E.A.S.T. Master these four vital areas to launch a global platform, build an audience, and deliver a powerful message to your ideal clientele.

ENTREPRENEUR
AUTHOR
SPEAKER
TRAINER

SUCCESS SPEAKS E.A.S.T. includes an Executive Membership in Success Speaks Global for a period of two years and lifetime access to Get Write University for Authors. Profit-sharing opportunities available. Only 10 spaces available per year.

Training includes group and individual sessions via video, written materials, and digital resources. Progress checkpoints will be conducted to ensure that each member succeeds over the course of the program.

At the end of the program, participants will have an opportunity to speak at a major business event, conduct a book signing, and launch a training program to an awaiting audience.

SuccessSpeaksEAST.com

GET WRITE UNIVERSITY

Rekesha Pittman's book publishing recipe has become legendary. Known as "The Midwife," Rekesha has successfully trained over 500 authors worldwide. Allow her expertise to work for you!

Enrollment Includes:
- Lifetime Access to the Course
- Video Lessons
- Visual Demonstrations
- Written Lessons
- Writing and Accountability Challenges
- Complete Modules at Your Own Pace
- Exclusive eBooks
- Scheduled LIVE Q&A Sessions

- An Interactive Community of Authors
- Special Discounts to Author Events Vending Opportunities

Access each training session on-demand and move at your own pace.

Learn needed skills for publishing process and watch them happen on your screen.

Participate in designated writing challenges and access author events.

GetWriteUniversity.com

Rekesha Pittman
Success Speaks Global

Rekesha Pittman is called "The Midwife" because she has helped visionaries worldwide launch both books and businesses. Rekesha is in-demand as a speaker and panelist for a wide variety of topics including publishing, speaking, and entrepreneurship.

Rekesha produces innovative webinars, creative curriculum, strategic coaching, and successful profit-making strategies via online training, speaking platforms, live workshops, and group educational sessions.

FOR BOOKING AND INQUIRIES

SuccessSpeaksGlobal.com

Email: **info@SuccessSpeaksGlobal.com**

SUCCESS SYSTEMS

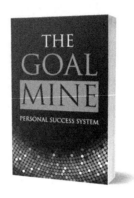

SuccessSpeaksGlobal.com

Made in the USA
Las Vegas, NV
04 June 2022

49798676R00036